Stock Market Investing

for

Beginners & Dummies

By: Giovanni Rigters

Table of Contents

Important Disclaimer

This book is presented solely for educational and entertainment purposes. The author is not offering it as legal, accounting, financial, investment, or other professional services advice. The content of this book is the sole expression and opinion of its author. It is not a recommendation to purchase or sell equity, stocks or securities of any of the companies or investments herein discussed. The author cannot guarantee the accuracy of the information contained herein. The author shall not be held liable for any physical, psychological, emotional, financial, or commercial damages, including, but not limited to, special, incidental, consequential or other damages. You are responsible for your own choices, actions, and results. Please consult with a competent tax and/or investment professional for investment and tax advice.

Introduction

It's time to get serious about your financial life and start thinking about the future. No one can and should work their whole life; you still want to enjoy life, spend quality time with your family and your body won't let you work forever. Also, nowadays you cannot rely on a pension-like in the "good ole days".

So, it's up to you and no one else to take the steps toward building your wealth. The process is not hard, but you will have to pay attention and spend some time learning about investing. There is no way around it.

There are many ways you can invest, and there are many different investment accounts on the market, but it is not too hard or complicated to weed through the investment jungle. It's also highly likely that you will start enjoying it and take it to the next level by investing in individual companies.

First, we have to start with the basics of what stocks are and what the stock market is. We'll delve into how to make money and what to do if there is a market crash. Then we'll look at some common misconceptions and mistakes people make in the stock market. So, follow along with me as we traverse this jungle on our way to paradise.

Chapter One: What Are Stocks? The Easiest Way to Get Rich!

A stock is simply put a piece of a company. A stock represents ownership and is an asset you can buy. The people who own these stocks are called shareholders.

Let's look at an example. If you and your family are going to eat a pie or pizza that has 8 slices then everyone will get at least one piece or slice. Out of the eight slices, you get only one and your Dad gets two.

You got one/eight or 12.5% of the pizza and your dad got 2/8 or 25%.

Companies work the same way, but instead of 8 shares of stock, they could have shares of stock in the millions or even billions.

McDonalds has 797 million shares outstanding. Walmart has 2.9 billion and Facebook has 2.3 billion shares outstanding.

Shares outstanding is a term used to explain the total amount of company shares on the stock market for shareholders to buy and sell amongst themselves. Shareholders can be people or different types of institutions.

Also, you are not limited by geography when investing, because you can buy stocks from companies around the world. So, if you want to buy stocks from companies in the Netherlands or even Brazil, you can.

One thing you need to pay attention to is that there are two types of stocks on the market, growth stocks, and income stocks.

Companies that see their stock price rise fast, like technology companies, are growth stocks, for example, Facebook and Twitter. These are rapidly growing companies and any income they make is put back in the company for further growth and expansion.

Income stocks, my favorite, are stocks that periodically pay their shareholders a dividend. This is usually quarterly, but it could also be monthly, semi-annually or annually.

The companies that can afford to pay their shareholders' income are large well-established companies, like Procter & Gamble or the Pepsi Company.

There are benefits to owning both growth and income stocks. Growth stocks have the potential to increase in value fast, but they are also more volatile and risky. Income stocks, on the other hand, provide a consistent stream of dividend income but the stock itself might not appreciate in value as fast as a growth stock.

For these two types of stocks, there are also two different types of investors, growth investors, and value investors.

Growth investors love it when they see their stock price increase in value, also called a capital gain.

They are also more willing to take on greater risk for an even greater reward.

Value investors like analyzing a company's metrics and numbers and are willing to wait until it's the right time to buy shares in a company. Value investors are good at discovering great companies who are consistent performers and are likely to stay consistent in the future based on the product or services they sell in the market they are in.

You might be thinking that to start buying stocks you need to have a ton of money or be a millionaire. That's not true at all, you can start by just buying one share in a company.

While I'm writing this, I saw that the Nike stock is being sold for $60, Coca-Cola for $46 and Twitter for $21. Now, this is not an endorsement to buy these three stocks. It's just an example that you don't need to spend thousands to get going.

Now with the boring definition complete, let's look at how people get rich with stocks.

The four main ways people can get rich are:

- capital gains
- dividends
- selling short
- options trading

The last two require a bit of skill and work and they are not as passive as the first two.

Capital gains are when your stocks gain in value. The beauty of this is that you do not perform any physical labor it's all passive.

Let's say you bought 10 shares of the $46 Coca-Cola stock on Tuesday so your stocks are worth $460. On Friday the stocks went up to $52.

Your stocks (**capital**) just increased (**gain**). Your investment is now worth $520.

So, your capital increased by $60. Now if you owned 100 or even 1000 shares that $6 increase would look even better.

With dividends you get rich by constantly buying dividend-paying stocks, reinvesting those dividends and you also enjoy the dividend increases from the companies themselves.

With dividends, it's more of a **Snowball Effect**. In the beginning, your income is low, but after time it exponentially increases allowing you to live off your dividend income without you ever having to sell your stocks.

Investing to get rich and wealthy should be your long-term goal.

Chapter Two: What is the Stock Market?

The stock market is like any other market where buyers and sellers come together to trade in goods or services.

Think about the car market. You're the buyer who is interested in buying a new red car. You will head over to the car dealership where you are met by eager salesmen. They show you the latest car models and after some back-and-forth, they convince you to put down some money in exchange for a new car.

The stock market or stock exchange works the same way, but instead of the car being the product its shares of stock.

The two most well-known stock exchanges in North America are the New York Stock Exchange and the NASDAQ. It's on these stock markets that you can buy shares in companies like Snapchat, Apple and Starbucks.

One of the main differences between the New York Stock Exchange and the NASDAQ is that the New York Stock Exchange offers traditional trading and the NASDAQ is electronic.

Traditional trading is face-to-face trading where buyers and sellers of stocks are on the trading floor executing orders. On the NASDAQ all orders happen electronically through computers and telephones.

Many small and up-and-coming companies can be traded over the counter or **OTC**. This is where investors can buy and sell penny stocks.

In the past, the stock markets were only available to the rich and wealthy among us. But ever since the doors **were** open to the common folk it has been one of the main vehicles in producing wealth.

There have been many times in history where the market crashed and people ended up losing all or most of their money. A stock market crash strikes fear in the hearts of many stockholders because many shareholders have their retirement and wealth invested in the stock market.

Why does the market go up and down and crash every couple of years? For an explanation, we have to look at both the short-term and long-term.

Short-term market fluctuations could be triggered by anything, like shareholder speculation, bad news about a sector, changes in governmental policies, companies meeting or exceeding their projected goals, and the list goes on.

I remember back in 2006 or 2007 there was a popular fast food restaurant in New York that was forced to shut down because the place had a rat infestation problem.

Even after it was closed, you could see the giant New York City rats run back and forth inside the restaurant.

Bad news like this made shareholders freak out and the company saw a decline in their share price.

After some time passed, the price of the stock climbed back up. You probably know which restaurant I'm talking about, but if you don't just do a quick search online, better yet use Youtube.

Fluctuations in the stock market are influenced by the market cycle we are in. During times of prosperity, the stock market is in a bull market meaning an upward trend.

In times of economic hardship and uncertainty, the stock market tends to be in a bear market, which is a downward trend.

Besides buying stocks you can also buy mutual funds, bonds, futures, options, commodities, index funds and ETFs on the market.

Companies on the stock market are all publicly traded companies. This means that these companies need to be transparent with their shareholders about their business activities.

They also need to present quarterly reports called 10Qs and yearly reports called the 10Ks along with an annual report.

To get listed on the stock exchange a private company on the primary market goes public through an **initial public offering** allowing its shares to be bought and sold on the secondary market, which is the market regular investors like you and I have access to.

A company only makes money during the IPO, by selling its shares to the public. It's then in the hands of the shareholders who can trade with each other.

Of course, a company keeps being the owner of a majority of their shares and they can buy back shares if it makes financial or business sense.

With all the different risks involved in the stock market, many people still invest in it, because long-term it has proven to be a great wealth builder.

Chapter Three: How to Buy Stocks

Before you jump in to buy one share of stock or multiple stocks, you need to have a goal you want to reach.

Are you investing for retirement? Do you want to buy stocks because you think you can make money fast? Or perhaps you just want to get your feet wet and just gain some experience.

Answering the thoughtful question, **what** your goal is, will determine what type of investor you will be, how much money you will need and how long you should hold on to the stocks you are planning on buying.

Answering this question will also determine if you are a short-term or long-term investor.

Short-term investors like to buy and sell frequently within the same day or a couple of weeks. These traders are called day traders and swing traders. These traders try to make money fast by buying low and selling high or short selling. They are in their trading accounts every single day the stock market is open, looking for opportunities to make a profit.

Long-term investors take a different approach. They still keep an eye on how their stocks are performing. But they take the long-term approach of buying stocks to hold for 5, ten or many more years. If you invest for retirement you would take the long-term approach.

You should also ask yourself how much risk you are willing to take on if you buy stocks. The stock market can be very volatile and you could lose a ton of money if you are not careful.

If you are a young investor who has some money to play around with and doesn't mind the short-term up and downswings of the market, then you can take on a good deal of risk.

But if you are close to retirement and want to preserve and grow your money then you should be more cautious about investing and buying stocks.

It's also a good idea to talk to a financial advisor or financial planner.

To start investing you need an investment account. This account gives you access to buy and sell equities also called stocks. There are many types of accounts on the market, but the more prominent ones are the 401k, IRA, Roth IRA, traditional brokerage account, the 403b, and the education savings account, also called ESA.

The 401k and 403b are available only through your employer if they decide to enroll in these accounts. Companies also offer a certain match percentage or dollar amount to motivate their employees to participate in the plans. There is a limit, however, to how much you can contribute to a 401k or 403b.

The IRA, which stands for an individual retirement account, and the Roth IRA are both retirement accounts you can set up with an investment firm, bank, or credit union.

Three differences between the IRA and 401k are the limit amounts, company match, and selection of investment options. IRAs and Roth IRAs always have a lower limit compared to the 401k, IRAs also do not offer a company contribution match.

Where IRAs and Roth IRAs do stand out is in allowing you to invest in whatever you like. Investing through a 401k is always limited by what the company has chosen for its employees, which are target-date retirement funds, a limited selection of mutual funds and index funds and no individual stocks to select from unless the company allows you to purchase some of its stock.

Also, you don't have to choose between setting up a 401k or IRA, because you are allowed to have both.

401k and IRAs penalize you if you withdraw your money before you are 59 and a half. You get hit with the 10% penalty and you are more than likely also going to pay taxes.

This is where the traditional brokerage accounts step in. The brokerage account allows you to withdraw your money anytime, but you will, however, pay taxes on your capital gains and dividends, but you won't get hit with a 10% penalty.

With all the different types of accounts on the market it might be hard to choose one to get started, so let me tell you what I've done. First, I enrolled in the 401k and got my company match, I then opened a Roth IRA with a discount broker and then I opened a traditional brokerage account. Don't forget you are not limited by the number of investment accounts you can have.

Some of the top brokerage firms are:

- Ally
- E-Trade
- TD Ameritrade

Opening an account is also, really easy. Just head over to the investment website and click on the "Open Account" button or you can also call them and they will eagerly help you in opening your account.

To buy stocks, you need to know the ticker symbol of the company you want to buy stock in. The ticker symbol is the unique abbreviation of the company on the stock market, for example, the Pepsi Company is found under the ticker symbol **PEP**, Amazon is **AMZN** and Walt Disney is **DIS**.

Once you know the ticker symbol you are ready to find out what the price of a share is and how many you want to buy. Head over to your brokerage account and log in, navigate to your trading option and type in the number of shares you want to buy.

In my example below, we are looking to buy 5 Coca-Cola stocks. Now you have to choose your order type. Let's go ahead and choose the market order, which means we'll buy the stock at whatever price it is on the market currently.

Action	Shares	Symbol	Price
⦿ Buy	5	KO	⦿ Market
○ Sell			○ Limit
○ Sell Short		☐ Find Stock Symbol	○ Stop
○ Buy to Cover		Preferred Stock Format	○ Stop Limit
			○ Market on Close
		Advanced Orders:	⬍

Preview Order
Disable Preview Step

You then preview your order where you can see what you are buying, how many shares, what your commission is, meaning your trading fee and your order total.

Please Review Your Order Carefully

Account: 38721198 - Individual Account

Action	Amount	Symbol	Description	Price	Duration	Qualifiers	
Buy	5 Shares	KO	COCA-COLA CO (THE)	Market	Day Order	None	Modify

Estimated Commission: $4.95
Estimated Order Total: $237.90

Place Order

Hit place order and if you're trading during the regular hours, which is Monday through Friday 9:30 a.m. Eastern Time, your order will execute immediately and your trading account will update with the stocks you just bought.

So, this is a fairly easy process. However, the important thing is to buy stocks at the right time by looking at both the technical and fundamental analysis of a company.

Chapter Four: The Stock Market Will Crash! Here's What You Should Do

A stock market crash occurs when there is a dramatic and swift decline in stock prices across many sectors or industries. This decline happens quickly in just a few days or can take some time to hit the bottom, so to say. This drop is so significant that the stock markets end up closing early to prevent the stock prices from declining even further.

A stock market **correction** should not be confused with a crash. A correction takes place when the market has been overvalued and needs to be adjusted by coming down to its respective valuation. Market corrections happen often and usually don't last very long, because when they have been readjusted, it's back to business as usual.

A crash, however, is when all hell breaks loose and the sky is falling. You'll hear newscasters preaching the end of the world and you'll see politicians blame one another's policies that led to the crash.

A stock market crash can be influenced by many events: like an economic depression or recession, instability in countries and stockholders' speculations bidding up shares so much that they form a stock market bubble.

This is purely emotional and all logic is out of the window. The bubble always ends up bursting and shareholders start selling in panic. When this happens, you need to stay calm of course; if you panic you will make mistakes.

The first thing to remember is that we've had crashes in the past. Each one has always been different, but we've been able to bounce back.

If you are a short-term investor then this is the right time to start **short selling**, which is the act of borrowing shares, selling them at the higher market price, than buying them back at a lower market price and finally returning those borrowed shares, the difference is your profit.

If you're retired or close to retirement, your money needs to be in safer fixed-income assets, so you should not feel too much of the sting. I'm talking about assets like bonds, cash, money market accounts, savings accounts, and annuities.

Only a small percentage needs to be in stocks. If you are a long-term investor, continue to stick to your investing strategy of consistently buying investments weekly, bi-weekly or even monthly.

What you are doing is called **dollar-cost averaging**. This is when you invest a fixed dollar amount periodically to buy investments. If you are investing through your employer in the 401k, then you are already participating in dollar-cost averaging, because the money that is taken out of your check is invested on a weekly, bi-weekly or monthly basis no matter what is happening in the market.

The benefit of this is that it takes out your emotions because your money is invested during the good times and the bad. So, you're buying investments when they are both expensive and cheap, which averages you out.

The biggest advantage to invest during a market crash is that you can buy stocks cheap. It's like going through your local store and you see everything is on sale for at least 40% off. So, those new black shoes you wanted are now 60% off. The new MacBook you're looking to buy … 50% off.

I know most people don't have the stomach to buy during a crash this is when dollar-cost averaging is your much-needed friend. Allowing you to buy equities while they are cheap also boosts your compound interest which is the interest you've received on your original investment amount, which is compounded with the latest interest just received.

So, in other words, you're making interest on your interest.

While everyone around you is panic selling at a loss and losing their investments, you're calmly buying more assets through dollar-cost averaging and undervalued individual stocks at an affordable price and holding on to them for the long term.

On a side note, make sure you hold on to your dividend-paying stocks because these companies are mostly well-established market leaders. When there is a crash they tend to bounce back quicker compared to non-dividend paying stocks, like most tech companies.

The dividend you receive from these companies also acts as a cushion to lessen the blow from the crash; companies like McDonald's, Pepsi and Nike continued to pay dividends even during the housing crash of 2008-09.

Let's look at two examples of stock market crashes. The first example is the crash of 1929 that led to the Great Depression. Different bankers, investment firms and traders participated in manipulating the markets by buying large chunks of highly overvalued stocks and then selling these to unsuspected retail investors. Investors like you and me.

Because these businesses bought a large number of shares, they were constantly pushing up the share prices. Individual investors saw their share prices skyrocket and kept purchasing more because there was no limit, they thought.

They even opened **margin accounts** letting them invest with borrowed money, offered by their brokerage firms. Most institutional investors did reap their rewards and jumped out of the market leaving the individual investors with overpriced stocks.

When the decline happened, everything went fast. Not only did people lose money, because they got hit with the **margin call** to return the money they borrowed, they also lost their jobs, their retirement wealth (which was of course invested in the stock market), and many people lost their minds.

The second crash we will take a look at is the dotcom crash of the early 2000s. The dotcom bubble was **based purely on speculation**. The internet was that new shiny object everybody wanted a piece off. Everybody and their Grandma tried setting up a website and then trading it on the secondary market through an IPO.

Many of these companies never could make a profit or were mostly in the red, but people did not care, websites were evaluated by how many clicks they received or how many eyeballs they could generate, instead of using traditional valuation methods, like revenue and expenses.

At the height of the bubble, everything came tumbling down, like a house of cards. Many startup companies received millions in venture capital funds with the impossible task to get just as big if not bigger than the tech giants of those days like Microsoft, Apple and Oracle.

Chapter Five: How to Make Money in the Stock Market

So, you want to make easy money in the stock market, but don't know where to start, how to take action or you're trying to figure out how other successful investors are making money.

We'll look at the two easiest ways investors have been able to get rich by investing in the stock market. Best of all, you can do it also. The two common ways investors make money in the stock market **are** with capital gains and dividends.

Capital Gains Explained

When you have your money invested in the stock market the value of this asset goes up and down. When your money, also called your capital, increases in value you have just received a **capital gain** and when it decreases in value it's called, you guessed it, a **capital loss**.

As long as your money is invested in the stock market it's **unrealized**. It only becomes realized once you sell your stocks.

Let's look at an example; you decide to buy 100 Nike shares at around $65. Without factoring in trading fees, you ended up buying $6,500. This is also what your Nike stock capital is worth is.

A few days go by and you decide to check on the stock's performance. You notice that the Nike stock price dropped from $65 to $61. So, your capital also dropped in value, from $6,500 to $6,100 to be exact.

You lost $400, which is your capital loss. But you thought about this chapter and remembered that this is an unrealized capital loss because it is still parked in the stock market. You decide to wait it out and after a few more days the stock price increased back to $65 and you're happy that you're at a break-even point.

After a few days, it hits $72. You have just experienced your first unrealized capital gain and decide to sell your Nike shares. You sell all your 100 shares at the current stock price of $72. So, you just received $7,200 in your cash account (transfer fees not accounted for). By selling you turned your unrealized gain into a realized capital gain.

$7200 - $6500 = $700, you just made a quick $700 without doing any physical labor.

Now, you still have to pay taxes on your capital gains depending on which type of investment account you were using and which income tax bracket you are in.

This quick explanation is how many day and swing traders **and even long-term investors** make money. They analyze stock charts by looking at indicators and patterns to decide when to buy and sell stocks.

You made a quick $700 with 100 Nike, but if you bought 1000 shares your profit would have been $7,000!

If you have the money to spare, don't like taking any risks and have idle time on your hands, you could make a pretty penny quickly by investing in the very risky penny stocks out there.

Dividends

The second most common method investors make money is with dividends they receive from dividend-paying stocks.

Let's stick with the Nike stock example. So, you bought 100 shares at $65, but instead of selling for a capital gain you decided to hold on to those stocks for 1 year. Nike has made four dividend payments of $0.18 per share for the year. With your 100 shares, you received $18 for every single quarter or $72 total.

The great thing about dividends is that these payments get deposited into your cash account or you can also reinvest them to buy more whole or fractional shares. These whole and fractional shares also end up paying you dividends.

There are also disadvantages to dividends. The money you receive from dividends is mostly a lot lower than you would receive from a capital gain. Dividends are also a long-term strategy, they are not get-rich-quick. Also, many companies are flaky with their dividend payments. Some constantly cut their dividend payments and others completely halt paying dividends during times of financial hardship. Some companies never increase their dividend payments or increase it after years of paying the same dividend amount.

However, I like dividend-paying stocks, but only from specific companies. I do fundamental research to see which companies are worth buying and I also analyzed the dividend payment history, especially during times of economic turmoil, because companies that can still pay an increasing dividend during a stock market crash are companies to keep an eye on.

Let's look at five dividend-paying stocks you should have on your watch list.

Number one: Nike - This athletic apparel retailer sells its products worldwide with a focus specifically on athletes. However, the brand is still so immensely popular that even non-athletic types also were Nike apparel. The biggest moneymakers are their footwear products, with their flagship Jordan brand always selling like hotcakes.

Number two: the Pepsi Company - Many consumers think that the Pepsi Company only owns the beverage, but they also own popular brands such as Frito-Lay and Quaker Foods. The Pepsi Company has done a great job diversifying its portfolio of brands with high-quality consumer goods.

Number three: Coca-Cola – This Company, which is one of the most recognized brands worldwide, owns many additional brands besides the iconic Coke brand, like Minute Maid, Vitamin Water, and Powerade.

Number four: Realty Income - This Real Estate Investment Trust (REIT) has tenants such as Walgreens, FedEx and LA Fitness. They operate nationwide and are also diversified across many different industries. They also pay a monthly dividend, which makes them a favorite dividend company for many investors.

Number five: Fastenal - This fairly boring company sells industrial and construction supplies. Even though Fastenal is not in an exciting industry like technology, it makes up for it by its sheer consistency in delivering value to both its customers and shareholders

Chapter Six: Dividends - Invest for Passive Income

If you want to invest for passive income, look no further than dividend-paying stocks.

We'll talk about what dividends are, why companies give them out to shareholders and the pros and cons. At the end, I'll give you four great dividend stocks to put on your watch list.

Dividends are a great way to earn a consistent income. Companies pay out dividends to their shareholders quarterly, but some companies pay out monthly, semi-annually or annually dividends.

When you receive a dividend, it is either deposited in your **cash account** or it is reinvested to buy more whole or fractional shares. This is also called a dividend reinvestment plan or **DRIP**.

The ultimate goal of a dividend strategy is to receive dividend payments that meet or exceed your **earned income**. It is at this moment that you can retire and live off dividend income without ever having to sell the underlying stocks.

It's also important that these dividend payments grow faster than inflation to maintain your buying power.

Do you need 1 million dollars to start investing in dividend-paying stocks? Of course not. You can start by just buying one or two shares in dividend-paying companies.

However, it will help if you have more money to invest because you'll get more in dividend income. The more shares you own the more dividends come your way.

For example, the Coca-Cola Company pays out a 37 cents quarterly dividend, which adds up to one dollar and 48 cents a year.

That's what you would receive if you only owned one Coke share, but if you owned 100 shares you would receive $148 for the year.

To see your dividends make an impact, there are three things to take into account.

Number one is, of course, buying dividend stocks consistently. Number two, the dividends you receive need to be reinvested or used to buy other shares that pay dividends and number three, the companies you invest in need to grow their dividends faster than inflation yearly.

These three factors will snowball your dividend income. Companies that pay dividends are usually blue-chip companies. These are well established and large companies. They are the top companies in their industry, companies like Walmart, 3M and Proctor & Gamble.

Because these companies are well established they tend to not experience a ton of growth, like a successful startup company.

Many of these blue-chip companies generate a ton of cash, which they end up paying out as a dividend to their shareholders.

Shareholders demand these dividends from companies as repayment for investing and believing in the company, but leadership in the company also benefits from dividend payments, because they get awarded stock shares and options.

So, let's say you have a successful local company selling ice cream and are planning to expand nationwide. You need more capital to achieve this, so you connect with investors who will invest in your company, but they want ownership in the form of stock shares.

Your company goes public and after 15 years you've been able to expand nationally. Your business is at a point where growth is slowing down.

Your investors who've held onto these shares want to receive some of their investment money back. So, you decide to pay dividends to your investors, so they can take their dividend income and invest it in a new business opportunity.

Keep in mind that not all companies pay a dividend, because every company goes through the business lifecycle.

Business Life Cycle

Size

Start-up   Growth   Maturity   Decline

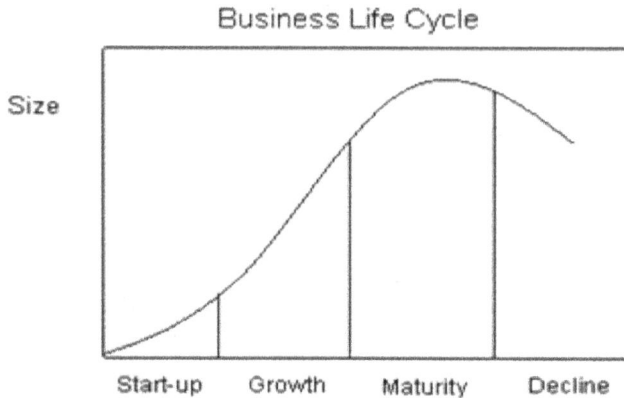

A business first starts as an idea in the mind of the creator. It is in this start-up phase where it can be a small group of people working together, believing in the idea of the creator.

It's also at this point where venture capitalists and angel investors could see the potential of the business.

After working out all the kinks and learning from their mistakes, the company should have a customer base. It now can enter the growth phase. In this phase there are still a lot of growing pains, this is also where a company might decide to go public and issue shares to potential shareholders.

All the revenue a company generates is invested back into the business to further grow the company, think about businesses like Snapchat.

A company eventually hits the maturity stage where it is well established and a leader in its space. It's at this stage cycle where most companies start to pay dividends to their shareholders, companies like

Walmart Clorox, ExxonMobil and even Johnson & Johnson.

Being a leader in your market is great, but if companies are not careful they can shift into the decline cycle where their products are becoming obsolete, like the Walkman or Polaroid pictures.

Some of the pros of dividend investing:

They are stable and consistent more so than capital gains. You benefit from the cash payment and also from the increase in the share price of the stock.

Because these companies are seen as more stable they tend to perform better during the stock market crash, because investors will sell their riskier stocks and look at more safe and stable companies and bonds to invest in.

You can also plan out your dividend income, which is harder to do with capital gains.

A couple of cons of dividend investing are: companies that pay out a dividend tend to appreciate slower in the stock market. Companies can also cut or even stop paying a dividend and some companies don't even grow their dividends.

It is therefore important to only invest in great dividend-paying companies, which will not only pay a healthy dividend but also have the financial capabilities to grow these dividends yearly.

Let's look at four of these companies:

Number one: Walmart - this retail giant has stores worldwide, saving its customers money by providing products at competitive prices. Lately, they've been focusing much more on their online presence. They bought jet.com and a delivery company to improve their same-day-delivery.

Number two: Lowe's - the second-biggest home improvement retailer, with of course Home Depot being number one. Lowe's has done such a good job in their field, they've been able to pay a consistently growing dividend for over 50 years!

Number three: McDonald's - the golden arches have been dragged through the mud, especially with the younger generation focusing more on healthier food and snacks. However, McDonald's is still the number one fast-food restaurant and this giant pays a quarterly dividend.

And number four: Fastenal - this boring company provides tools and equipment for businesses to create products, build and maintain facilities and they also sell safety products for personnel. Fastenal not only has a great business, they also have repeat customers. Nothing is more important for a company then having customers that constantly return to buy your products.

Chapter Seven: 90% of Investors Make These 5 Mistakes

Making a mistake will make you scratch your head and think about what you've done wrong. But making additional mistakes will surely make you want to quit.

I want to prevent this from happening by letting you know what the five common mistakes are that investors make, so you won't fall for them.

Number one: the so-called Financial or stock market gurus

These are the so-called personalities who tell you what to buy and when to sell. They might also end up screaming their predictions.

You should always be cautious when someone is giving you investing advice. Sometimes there are financial incentives that come into play in advising you what to buy.

Always question the information you receive and that your guru has those investments he or she is pitching to you in their portfolio. Gurus know how to tap into people's fears and emotions to get them to take action.

Following the herd is also very risky. Instead of following a guru you're following along everybody else. So, if there are family members or even colleagues at work who will tell you what to buy and sell, you listen to them without even doing your research first.

This is very dangerous and this is how people lose their money, by listening to hot tips.

You don't want to follow the herd, they're easily influenced and they act on emotions only when it comes to investing in the stock market. The herd is not logical, whatsoever, and they only follow the latest trends hoping to get rich quick.

Number 2: not being patient and expecting wealth immediately

People invest in the stock market to get rich, save for retirement or maintain the wealth they have accumulated. Being impatient and expecting results too soon will leave you disappointed and open to make mistakes.

Every one of us has heard stories about investors making millions out of small investments. Most of these stories are anomalies because the vast majority of investors have to invest for the long-term to see significant gains in their investments.

Of course, it is possible to make a ton of money fast, but that is also very risky. The higher the risk in your investment the higher the potential reward could be, but it could also be your downfall.

Number 3: not enjoying the investing process

You don't need to be passionate about investing to make it work in your favor, but you need to have some interest in investing. If the thought of doing your due diligence to decide which companies to invest in does not spark your interest, then it is best to invest passively which is investing in mutual funds, ETFs or index funds.

There is absolutely nothing wrong with being a passive investor and it's also recommended for beginning investors.

That's how I started, by investing in mutual funds, bonds, and index funds. I quickly learned that investing was not too hard and I thought it was kind of interesting. I then switched from being a passive investor to being an active one, researching individual companies I want to invest in, buying them when they are undervalued and making sure my asset allocation is up to date.

Number four, giving up too early on the market

Many of us have had a bad experience with the market or know someone who has.

Stock market crashes occur far too frequently, leaving investors disappointed, frustrated and stressed out.

Many investors also get scammed into investing in shady companies, which end up crashing on the stock market. Like my dad, who got contacted by an investment firm to invest in this particular mutual fund poised for growth.

He ended up losing all his money and swore never to invest again. Luckily, I've been able to show him the error of his ways and he has become an avid investor. I need to slow him down from not buying too many stocks, especially when they are overvalued.

If you're ready to give up, DON'T. Try to figure out what you did wrong and ask for help if you need to. The stock market is still one of the best ways to build wealth.

Number 5: jumping in with no goals

Goals are your road map to success. Without a map, you will never be able to reach your destination. Imagine traveling from Kansas to New York without a map. You will have a much more pleasant travel experience with your map in your reach.

This also applies to investing. You need to have a goal. Are you planning on day trading for a living? Or do you want to invest in penny stocks? Maybe you're investing time horizon is only 10 years.

These things will influence your investment strategy. It's okay to start and test the waters without a plan in the beginning. But you quickly find out that you need a long-term goal which will have a major impact on your asset allocation.

Chapter Eight: 5 Lies You've Been Told About Investing

There are many lies people have been told about investing. Some of these lies **are** self-thought. People have been lied to because the person telling this lie doesn't know any better or they failed themselves and don't want to see you fail.

Other people have succeeded and don't want to see you accomplish your goals. So right now, we'll debunk 5 lies you've been told about investing.

Number one: you need to be a millionaire or have a lot of money to start investing

This is not true at all in this day and age. Yes, in the past the stock markets were only for the rich and wealthy, but the doors have been opened to us common folks a long time ago.

With the help of the internet investing the stock market is a lot more accessible now. You can buy and sell shares from the comfort of your living room or bedroom. Discount brokers have also made it very affordable to buy and sell shares. Previously, you would have to pay hundreds of dollars just to buy or sell stocks. Now your commission fee can be as low as $4.99 or even free if you're using an app like **Robinhood**.

You also don't need thousands of dollars to buy shares. You can start by just buying one share in a company like Coca-Cola, which has a share price of $46 right now.

It's also better to start with a little bit of money compared to investing $1 million from the get-go. The reason for this is that with small amounts of money you can experiment and have fun while you're learning the ins and outs of the market.

Imagine your first time investing with $1 million; you would probably be too scared or cautious with the money hoping not to lose a single penny in the market.

Number 2: I don't have enough or make enough money to start investing

Now, this one is a follow-up from the last lie. Any small amount of money you can set aside will help, even if it's only $10 a week. These 10 dollars add up to $520 by the end of the year and you can start investing with $520. Start saving for investing now and your future self will thank you.

Look at where you could save a couple of dollars during the week. It might mean eating out less during the week or one less trip to Starbucks a week. That is if you like Starbucks of course.

A change of mindset will do wonders. Instead of saying I don't have $10 to spare, change it to how can I save $10 a week? You will kick your subconscious into high gear and before you know it you'll end up saving even more than just $10 a week.

Number 3: invest now because long-term the market has always seen a 7% return

Number three is a tricky one. You will hear financial advisors and even people in the media saying this one. The reason you have to be careful with this one is that the future is unpredictable.

No one can predict what the market will do or return in a given year. If the market went up 10% last year that does not mean that it will go up another 10% in the future. On the flip side, however, staying on the sidelines, because you don't know what the market will do is risky in itself.

People usually talk about long-term returns to ease your mind and get you into investing. If you stay on the sideline not only will your money not grow, it's losing its buying power, because of yearly inflation.

Number four: I don't invest because the stock market is too risky

This one follows up nicely with lie number 3. Yes, if you don't have at least some basic knowledge about investing then it will be too risky, but with the help of financial planners and advisors, there's no need to be scared. Also, many investors do at least some self-education by reading investing books and listening to some audiobooks.

Keep in mind that there is risk involved with anything you do. If you don't want to invest and rather keep the money under your mattress, you are opening yourself up to burglars, house fires or even your dog that might end up eating or shredding your money.

If you think that leaving your money in the bank or your savings account is the way to go, think again. With the measly 1% or less in interest that you earn, your money's buying power is being eaten away by inflation.

If on average inflation is 3% per year, $1 today is worth 3% less next year, so $0.97.

Number 5: You need to be an expert to start investing

You indeed need to have some basic knowledge about how the stock market works, but you don't need to be Warren Buffett to get started. Get yourself educated by reading books (this one is a great start).

Once you have built up your confidence, you can start by investing a small amount of money. Money you would not mind losing. By investing a little amount, you psychologically prepare yourself for growth, because once you see your investments growing it will build up your confidence and knowledge to invest more, in a responsible manner of course.

I hope I've been able to motivate you by debunking some of the most common lies that I often hear being told to eager investors.

Chapter Nine: 25 Stock Market Investing Tips

Before you start investing, you might have a couple of questions or concerns. I've listed 25 of the most common things I've noticed from new investors and how to set yourself up for success. Let's get started!

Write down your goals

If you don't know where you are going, there is no need to even get started. Make sure to write down your investing goals and be specific with the timeline.

Do you want to have $500k in your retirement account in 15 years? Or do you want to have $1 million in 10 years?

What will your investment strategy be to acquire this wealth? And what will your portfolio mix of securities look like? Will your portfolio consist of 70% stocks 25% bonds and 5% cash?

Writing down your goals will give you a clearer picture of what you want to accomplish and how to do it.

Start investing early

The earlier you start investing, the faster will not only your money grow, but you'll also be able to retire quicker (depending on your financial goal).

How early should you start? When you get your very first job. It does not matter if this is a retail job or one waiting tables at a restaurant. You want to get into the habit of thinking about your future now and setting aside money to invest, so you won't have to work for the rest of your life.

Starting your investing journey at an early stage in your life also has the benefit of seeing how your money grows, which will give you the confidence to invest even more.

Inflation eats away at your money

You might refrain from investing in the stock market because you've heard how risky it can be and how many people have lost a lot of money in it.

But, keeping your money under your mattress or even in a savings account is also very risky, because of inflation.

Inflation is the rise in the cost of goods which lowers the value of money. A chocolate bar today might cost $1, but next year it could cost $1.05. So that same dollar you have today is worthless in the future because it has **declining buying power.**

The stock market allows your money to not only keep its buying power, but it also can grow your money faster than inflation.

Do your research

It's not only good but necessary to do your research to see what businesses and companies you are investing in on the stock market. Almost everything you need to know about different stocks, bonds, and mutual funds can be found for free on the internet. I would refrain from paying any money to get stock market information.

The last thing you want is to invest in a scam or a company that is losing money and not making a profit, which could cause you to lose money in the long run. This happens to a lot of unsuspecting investors.

To start doing your research, all you would need is the ticker symbol of your investment to get started. A ticker symbol is the abbreviation of the company, mutual fund, index fund, bond, etc., on the stock market. You can then use a site like Morningstar.com to do your research.

Create your own rules

Good rules in investing give you boundaries to work in. If you have a rule not to invest in any company without doing some research on it first, you will save yourself a ton of headaches.

No one will be able to scam you with hot stock tips they have heard through the grapevine. This is how many people get scammed and bamboozled.

Good rules give you a level of confidence when you invest. It gives you that extra push when you are hesitant when buying new stocks or investments. They give you structure and a blueprint to stick to.

You can start with simple rules and add more complex rules once you get more experience with investing.

Example of rules:

60% of my investment portfolio will consist of stocks

I will only invest in companies that have been able to increase their earnings by at least 5% for the last ten years.

I will rebalance my portfolio yearly.

Don't listen to everyone

Be wary of who you take advice from. Some people, especially in the media, receive financial incentives to tell you what to invest in.

Also, family and friends could give you bad investing advice if they've heard about a "hot stock tip" at their job without doing any research first.

Keep in mind, just because you have heard of a popular company or use its products does not mean it could be a good investment.

Many companies in the stock market never turn a profit. A popular company, like Tesla that trades on the stock market under the ticker symbol TSLA, is still not profitable. Even though it's bringing in an increasing amount of revenue, its net income is still in the red.

Constantly educate yourself

I've always told myself that if you are uneducated on a topic like investing, then people will probably take advantage of you. It's very easy to set up an investment account with a big bank or even a retirement account at your job. But you should know what your investment options are, what you will be investing in and what types of fees you will be paying.

Nickle and diming you on fees could end up costing you thousands or even hundreds of thousands over your investing journey.

You should also have a basic understanding of how stocks, bonds, mutual funds, index funds, and other investment vehicles work. See three examples below:

When you purchase a stock or share, you are buying ownership in a company. Big companies like Apple, have shares outstanding in the billions. So, when you buy just one or two shares of stock, you only own a very small piece of the company.

Bonds are like IOUs that a company or government entity gives to you after buying the bond. When you buy a bond, you are going into a legal contract that states that not only will you get your original money back, you will also receive frequent interest payments.

A mutual fund is a fund that pools different investors their money and invests this in a variety of securities.

Have savings

Always have some money saved up for emergencies. Never invest all of your money. There is always a risk that you could lose all your invested money.

Make sure you have some money saved for emergencies, housing, entertainment/food, to start your own business, and college.

Don't forget that life is not predictable, your car might break down or you could get into an accident costing you much in medical bills. You can never be prepared, but you can have some money set aside.

Diversify your investments

Don't invest all your hard-earned money in one company. That's extremely risky unless you are a risk-taker (big risk, big reward type of person).

Make sure that the money that you do invest is diversified, meaning that you don't have all your money invested in one stock. A mutual fund could be a good solution for you.

Mutual funds allow you to pool your money with other investors and invest it in a variety of securities.

About a decade or two ago there was a company called Enron that went bankrupt after it was found out the company was lying about their earnings and profits. Many employees of Enron had all their retirement money invested in the company. When Enron went bankrupt, many employees ended up losing their retirement income, also. Imagine being in your 50s and your investment goes up in smoke.

That's why it's always smart to diversify.

Don't be emotional

Investing can be a literal emotional roller coaster ride. The daily up and downticks of the stock market can easily make you go crazy. One way to overcome this fear is to invest in what you are confident in.

This confidence comes with knowledge, patience and time. Knowing and accepting that investing has risk associated with it and you could lose money prepares you mentally for any downswings you might see happening in the stock market.

Don't rely on luck and miracles

If you look at the stock market as your way to get rich fast, then you could be setting yourself up for failure. Don't get me wrong, it is possible to take $10k, invest it, and turn it into millions because it has been done before.

But this investing strategy is extremely risky and most people are better equipped to mentally handle the longer and slower process of getting wealthy.

Assume that you can lose it all

If I can lose it all, why would I invest in the first place? Well, there is a reason why I added this tip. First of all, you are not supposed to have all your money in the stock market.

When you are younger you can take more risks, because you can bounce back from early losses. But when you are at your retiring age, you should think about investing in more conservative securities that might not increase in value as fast as stocks, but they will keep your money from not depleting.

Two of these securities are bonds and annuities.

Have side hustles

Besides having a job or a career and your investments, what else are you doing to bring in some additional money? In today's society job security is at an all-time low and many people are either unemployed, underemployed, or working part-time to pay the bills.

It's in your benefit to have some additional money streams. You could work part-time to make some extra money, but the main ones to think about are investment properties, dividend stocks, royalties (for example, from book sales), and your own business.

If you have a passion, like photography, drawing, or video editing, you could do some freelance work on the side and possibly turn it into a full-time venture. Always keep your eyes open for opportunities.

The best time to start is right now

I always get complaints from older people that they have missed the boat and they are too old to start investing. This is not true at all, it does not matter if you are 20 or 50, it's very important to invest, even if you start with a small amount.

There is always an opportunity to make good money in the stock market. However, that does not mean that you should start day trading with the money you do have invested if you are older to "catch up". This is just a recipe for disaster, as you will be way too emotionally involved to make the right trading choices.

Dividend investing

I'll let you in on a little secret. I only invest in dividend-paying companies which increase their dividends faster than inflation.

Dividends are earnings a company pays out to its shareholders. To get a dividend, you need to own at least one stock in a dividend-paying company.

These dividends not only increase my wealth over time, but they also give me peace of mind, because of their steady stream of income.

I not only enjoy the dividend, but I also see my stock increase in value. Now, I only buy these stocks when they are **undervalued**, which means they are trading under their market value.

Examples: Realty Income, McDonalds, TROWE Price

Growth investing

A growth investor is an investor who likes to buy low and see their investments grow. They eventually sell at a higher price than what they bought their investment for. The majority of investors are growth investors.

Technology stocks are good stocks to keep an eye on because these tend to increase in value very fast.

Examples: Facebook, Oracle, Microsoft

Start small

One complaint I hear is people telling me, "If I only had a million dollars I could start investing."

Not only is this not true, because you can start investing with as low as $10, it is also recommended to start small.

The biggest reason to start small is to get comfortable with investing. If you started by only investing let's say $100 and you see your money constantly rise and drop, it's fun to look at it your investment performance daily.

You will also start to gain the confidence and knowledge to invest smarter, which will lead you to invest bigger amounts.

Now, let's look at that from the other end. Let's say you inherited $1million and you have the task to invest this money. You have never invested before because you always told yourself that you needed more money and now you finally have it.

Guess what, you will be too scared to invest a million dollars. You don't have the expertise and the know-how.

If you started out investing small amounts for years and suddenly got this $1 million deposited in your lap, you will have the confidence to invest this amount, because you've already seen what works and what does not while you were investing small amounts.

Live your life

Never let the stock market control your daily life. The daily up and downswings of the market affect plenty of investors. When the market is at an all-time high, investors feel good, go to work in a good mood and go to sleep with a clear mind.

But when the market tanks, many investors feel like they just got kicked in the stomach. They are sad, angry, irritated and just in a very bad mood.

Also, don't become so frugal that you only want to invest all your money in the stock market and tell yourself that you will live a fun life when you are retired.

If you want to go on a vacation or buy yourself something nice, go ahead and do it.

Stick to what makes you comfortable

Everyone has their comfort zone when it comes to investing. Some people a risk-takers and would do well investing in penny stocks or day trading. Other investors are more conservative and would rather invest in securities that are not too risky and which allow them to preserve their wealth.

Always stick to what is comfortable for you. If you do not like to analyze and choose individual stocks to invest in, it's probably best to invest in mutual funds or index funds.

If you are someone who would rather not invest on your own and need some help, an investment firm that offers a full brokerage service is probably best for you.

Just make sure to always push yourself to learn more about investing, because at the end of the day this is your money and you are ultimately responsible for your retirement.

Have fun

I'll be the first to tell you that investing can get quite boring and uninteresting. Some people just don't like to analyze companies and look at financial numbers.

You should try to figure out what you like most about investing and hone in on that specifically.

Maybe you like to see your money grow, or maybe you like to see your dividend income increase month over month, you might also like other ways to make money such as selling short or options trading. Whatever it is, try to have fun with investing

Use technology to your advantage

We are very lucky that we can use our laptops or even a small device like our mobile phone to buy investments or to research stocks. The advancement of technology has also made it very affordable and fast to buy investments.

This means you can trade shares of stock no matter where in the world you are. All you need is an internet connection.

In the old days, you would have to call your broker and pay a very high commission to put in an order. Nowadays you have apps, like Robinhood, that are commission-free.

You also do not have to sign up for a full brokerage account. You can go with a discount broker, like Ally.com that has low trading fees.

Study the greats

Warren Buffett, Benjamin Graham, Charlie Munger? Make sure you read books on investing billionaires, how they amassed all their wealth and what they do to maintain it.

This will get you in the mindset of how the very rich think and conduct themselves. It will also show you how some have turned small amounts of cash into big wealth. Everyone likes rags to riches stories.

Don't fall in love with your investments

Every investment will be sold if it is not performing how it should be. This is one of my rules. I do not get my personal feelings mixed with investing.

It's fun to tell your family and friends that you own Disney or even Pepsi stock, but if these stocks don't make me any money, I end up selling them.

This is why I like to analyze a company's financials (annual reports), to see if they are still financially sound

Know what you are investing in

Before you follow anyone's advice, especially from any financial planners, make sure you know what you are investing in. There are many scammers out there who like nothing more than a clueless person they can take advantage of by using some industry terms to sound educated on the topic.

If you are investing in a mutual fund or even an ETF, make sure you get the ticker symbol of this entity to do some research on the companies you are investing in.

Some investors don't like to invest in weapon companies or prisons, but if you are investing in popular index funds, you are more than likely also investing in these institutions. Also, if a company is not conducting themselves ethically, would you still want to invest in them?

Break the rules

I just told you to create your rules and now I'm already telling you to break those rules? Yes, here's why. You should always experiment with your investing strategy. It is good to have rules, but now and then you might have to break them.

Investing should be fun and if you are stuck to rigid rules, it could become boring very quickly. The trick is to break the rules, but take small risks.

For example, you want to start investing in Cryptocurrency, but you have a rule not to invest in high-risk securities.

You have a gut feeling that you will do well with this investment. Go ahead and buy a small amount of cryptocurrency. Don't go all out and spend 50% of your portfolio in buying this currency.

Share your knowledge

Once you have some knowledge under your belt from investing in the stock market, you have your golden rules, and you are confident in your investing skills, you should share your knowledge with others.

You can start by educating your family and friends to get them comfortable with investing.

Surprisingly, there are many misconceptions about investing and many people have been burned multiple times investing in wrong stocks. This usually ends up scarring them for life and they will not lay a hand on any investments anymore.

This is where you can come in and show them how you have been successfully investing.

Believe me, it feels good to be able to help a family member and secure their financial future. Talking to people about your experience with investing will also allow you to meet like-minded investors who will take your investment skills to the next level.

Resources

Following is a list of free internet sources you can use for research:

Morningstar.com

Gurufocus.com

StockCharts.com

Finviz.com

Finance.Yahoo.com

Google.com/Finance

Keep in mind just to use the free version.

Chapter Ten: Residual Income Ideas (bonus chapter)

Let's look at three methods to make residual income which will skyrocket you to financial freedom.

If you are dying to quit your job, live the life you deserve or just simply want to have more freedom to do what you want, then you will like this chapter. Residual income is income you generate passively. So, the money continues to come your way no matter if you're not working or even sleeping.

I'm not going to lie to you and say that it's easy to get a residual income stream setup, but it is worth it. Because once you have this residual income stream setup, you only need to passively maintain it.

Online Businesses

The first method of making a residual income is by running an online business. This can be making money from ads while your blogging or making money from your YouTube channel. You can also set up your e-commerce site or sell other companies' products and get a commission, which is also called affiliate marketing.

Another popular way of making a residual income is from receiving royalty checks by selling physical books, eBooks, music or photos. Even though you can make money with these ideas, there is a ton of competition, because online businesses are very popular and people underestimate how hard it is to make a decent amount of money from these ideas.

With all the competition it also means that the online markets are flooded with mediocre products and services. So even if you come on the scene with the best product on the market you won't stand out. This is when you have to think about how you want to advertise your products or services to rise above all the other mediocre products and become the leader in your field.

Let me emphasize that having a product or service alone is just half the work. You also need to get visibility by advertising, whether this is social media marketing, PPC marketing or word of mouth marketing is up to you.

It's always good to do some competitive analysis and see how your competition is promoting their products.

Another problem with online businesses is longevity. Many of these businesses can be here today and gone tomorrow because the competition just pushed you out of the market, your products or services became obsolete or you could not keep up with technological or advertising changes, not allowing you to get all the necessary exposure to stay relevant. So, it's not set it and forget it, it's said it and maintain it.

Anything that is not considered passive I left out of the list. So, freelancing and consultancy only works while you are physically present, if not you won't get paid. This defeats the purpose of making residual income.

Real Estate

The second way to make a residual income is through real estate. I'm not talking about flipping houses because that takes too much work to buy and sell. It's also not passive.

The focus should be on income properties which cash flow. Meaning that after all expenses are accounted for you to come out with a net profit.

Your tenants are paying you rent monthly. With these rent payments, you pay down the mortgage (if any), home insurance, taxes, capital expenditures, etc. If you buy in the right location hire the right property manager and run your numbers, you can have a nice stable income.

You won't break the bank by just buying one property starting out and the more properties you buy and take a mortgage on will increase your debt amount. This accumulation of debt will also hinder your process of getting approved for additional loans.

This is when you have to get creative with financing your purchases. Private lenders or portfolio lenders could be two options to try out.

The rent payments allow you to generate residual income and the more properties you own the higher your residual income could potentially be.

There are also many tax benefits associated with doing real estate. This is not a method of making a ton of residual income fast, but it is stable and grows nicely with each additional property. Many millionaires owe their riches to real estate, also giving them the flexibility and freedom to travel and be their own boss.

A great way to start is to buy single-family homes, duplexes, triplexes or quads. These are considerably cheaper than commercial real estate or apartment complexes.

You can start with residential real estate or try your hands at franchising and commercial real estate once you have the skills and money saved up.

Dividend-Paying Stocks

The third method and if you have been paying attention to my book, you know what it is: making residual income through dividend-paying stocks.

There is a group of companies that pay some of their net income out as a dividend to shareholders. Not all of these companies are worth investing in, though. So, analyzing a company's performance is highly recommended.

The beauty of investing for dividends is that you are creating a nice stream of residual income that should grow faster than inflation. Companies increase their dividend payments and by constantly buying the right dividend stocks and reinvesting those dividends to buy whole or partial shares you supercharge your dividend income.

Just keep in mind that you will have to pay taxes on your dividend income depending on the type of investment account you're using.

It's also very easy to start because you don't need to have a ton of money. You can start by just buying one share of a dividend-paying company.

Many of the wealthiest individuals on earth have dividend-paying companies in their portfolio. Guys like Warren Buffett, Charlie Munger and even Bill Gates.

Now, the last two methods of making residual income, real estate and investing, I call those old money, because they have been the pillars of generating and maintaining wealth.

Online businesses, however, can be tricky. One month you could be making a lot of money, but the next month could be the total opposite. If you want to play it smart and safe, you should diversify your income streams, so you have money coming in from different sources.

Chapter Eleven: Conclusion

As a beginner, investing in the stock market can be quite daunting, so don't get hung up if you feel like you are lost. I've been there and many successful investors also felt this way when they bought their first shares. Once you take that leap of faith it will get easier.

It is also best to start investing with a small amount of money and monitor your results. This will give you the confidence and motivation to move forward. Once you have some experience under your belt, you can start taking calculated risks.

As always, you do need to constantly educate yourself, otherwise, you will make mistakes. But just the simple fact that you have made it this far, tells me that you are willing to do what is necessary to improve your financial future.

You have what it takes to become successful and take charge of your future with confidence.

Thank You

I would like to thank you from the bottom of my heart for coming along with me on this investing journey. There are many investing books out there, but you decided to give this one a chance.

If you liked this book, then I need your help!

Please take a moment to leave an honest review of this book. This feedback gives me a good understanding of the kinds of books and topics readers want to read about and it will also give my book more visibility.

Leaving a review takes less than one minute and is much appreciated.

Other Titles by Giovanni Rigters

50 Tips on Saving Money

Ever have a feeling that you never have enough money when needed? Would you like to have some extra cash to buy what you feel like?

Well, in this book we will look at 50 different tips allowing you to have so extra cash in your pocket and bank account.

Smart Investors Create Wealth

It's never too early to start your journey towards accumulating wealth. No one wants to work for the rest of their life.

I will show you what wealthy people have known for centuries on how to not only create wealth but also maintain it so you can pass it down.

www.ingramcontent.com/pod-product-compliance
Lightning Source LLC
Chambersburg PA
CBHW071514210326
41597CB00018B/2751